Ancient Order of United Workmen, Grand Legion of the Select Knights

Session Reports of the Grand Officers and Committee on Finance

with an appendix containing the reports of the Deputies

Ancient Order of United Workmen, Grand Legion of the Select Knights

Session Reports of the Grand Officers and Committee on Finance
with an appendix containing the reports of the Deputies

ISBN/EAN: 9783337223571

Printed in Europe, USA, Canada, Australia, Japan

Cover: Foto ©Andreas Hilbeck / pixelio.de

More available books at **www.hansebooks.com**

GR LEGION OF ONTARIO.

S OF A. O. U. W.

SSION 1889.

PORTS OF TE

GND OFFICERS

HE COMMITTEE ON FINANE

With ndix containing the Reports of
the Deputies.

T. CATHARINES :

OD, BOOK AND JOB PRINTER.

188.

REPORT

——OF THE——

Grand Commander

To the Officers and Members of the Grand Legion, Select Knights of the A. O. U. W. of Ontario.

COMRADES,—We are again called together to transact business connected with our institution and recognizing our allegiance to the Great Commander and Supreme Ruler of the universe, let us look for his guidance in all our transactions. We have great reason for thankfulness, that out of a Beneficiary Membership of over 1500 members we have had only three deaths during the term and one claim from disability. Notwithstanding this low assessment rate, the uncertainty as to our future has hindered our progress during the year and I sincerely hope such wise legislation may be enacted this session as may lead to great prosperity in the year we are about to enter upon.

I herewith present my report for the term and earnestly hope my official acts may meet your approval.

CIRCULARS.

I issued the following official Circulars :—

GRAND LEGION OF ONTARIO, S. K. OF THE A. O. U. W.

HEADQUARTERS OF THE GRAND COMMANDER.

PICTON, ONTARIO, August 1st, 1889.

To the Officers and Members of the Subordinate Legions under the Jurisdiction of the Grand Legion of Ontario.

COMRADES :—I desire to thank you for the honor you have conferred on me, by placing me in the high and honorable position of Grand Commander for the current year. It affords me great pleasure to be able to say that peace reigns in our Order and we enter on this year with every reason to anticipate a prosperous one, provided Officers and Members recognize their individual responsibility and every man does his duty by regular attendance at all meetings of his Legion and by encouraging others to join.

Regarding the Beneficiary Department of this Grand Legion there has been a want of promptness on the part of members in the paying of their assessments on or before the last day of the month, consequently the Grand Recorder and Finance Committee have not been in a position to meet claims as promptly as might be reasonably expected.

The small sum of Three Dollars was all that was required to pay every Assessment in the Department from the first of January to the end of May this year and this surely should have been paid before the last day of each month in which a call was made.

Section 6, of Article XI Grand Legion Constitution provides, that "any Legion failing or declining to make returns so as to insure their receipt by the Grand Recorder not later than the 7th of each month, shall again be notified by the Grand Recorder by registered letter and should such returns fail to be made witnin ten days from date of second notice, all certificates under the jurisdiction of said Subordinate Legion shall stand suspended until said returns are made." This clause in future must be enforced, so as to secure prompt payment of Beneficiary claims.

I would also call your attention to the action of the Grand Legion in ordering that the urinal test must be made in the case of such applicants for Beneficiary Certificates as are over forty-five years of age. I therefore request all Local Medical Examiners to make such examination.

I have made the following appointments :

GRAND MARSHALL.

Cde. W. D. McLaren, Jr......................Montreal.

COMMITTEE ON FINANCE.

Cde. James Watt, Chairman ....Toronto.

COMMITTEE ON LAWS AND THEIR SUPERVISON.

Cde. D. F. McWatt, Chairman ....Barrie
" O. C. Graves......................................St Catharines.
" G. A. McMullen ....Brockville.

DISTRICT DEPUTY GRAND COMMANDERS.

City of Montreal...............Cde. E. W. Beuthner of Montreal.
For York County .... " Wm. Wyndow " Toronto.
" Wentworth " .... " J. H. Shouldice " Hamilton.
" Lincoln " .... " J. W. King, Jr. " St. Catharines.
" Welland " .... " Hy. Emrick " Intern. Bridge
" Haldimand " .... " R. E. Walker " Caledonia.
" Norfolk " .... " J. Thos. Murphy " Simcoe.
" Oxford " .... " C. E. Burgess " Burgessville.
" Elgin " .... " M. D. Carder " St. Thomas.
" Essex " .... " D. Nicholson " Amherstburg.
" Kent " .... " J. E. Peers " Chatham.
" Middlesex " .... " A. McLean " Ilderton.
" Wellington " .... " D. Scroggie " Guelph.
" Bruce " .... " Robt. Millons " Walkerton.
" Perth " .... " J. A. Burgess, M.D." Listowel.
" Peel " .... " Edw. Stonehouse " Brampton.
" North Simcoe " .... " John Nettleton " Collingwood.
" South " " .... " R. Henderson " Alliston
" Dufferin " .... " E. Berwick " Shelburne
" Ontario " .... " R. S. Cormack " Whitby.
" Durham " .... " Chas. Keith " Bowmanville.
" Lennox " .... " H. V. Fralick " Napanee.
" Northumber'd " .... " W. Toms, Jr. " Cobourg.
" Frontenac " .... " W. K. Routley " Kingston.
" Prince Edwa'd" .... " F. C. Spencer " Wellington.
" Leeds " .... " J. Cumming " Lyn.
" Grenville " .... " W. G. Robinson " Prescott.
" Dundas " .... " C. Robson " Iroquois.
" Carleton " .... " J. J. Hamilton " Ottawa.
" Addington " .... " Jas. Aylsworth " Tamworth.
" Waterloo " .... " John Zryd " Hespeler.

In conclusion I hope the pleasant relations I have had with my Comrades ever since I became a member of the Order may be continued and that the year commenced so favorably may be one of progress, not trusting alone to our own efforts but looking for guidance and support from the Supreme Commander of the Universe in whom we all profess to trust and to whom we have each promised obedience.

I am   Yours fraternally in E. I. & U.,

WM. J. PORTE, *Grand Recorder.*

ATTEST : B. J. LEUBSDORF, *Grand Recorder.*

GRAND LEGION OF ONTARIO S. K. OF THE A. O. U. W.

HEADQUARTERS OF THE GRAND COMMANDER.

PICTON, ONTARIO, DECEMBER 15th, 1888.

To the Officers and Members of the Subordinate Legions under the Jurisdiction of the Grand Legion of Ontario.

COMRADES :—The year 1888 is now near its close and I desire to call your attention to the fact that while our Beneficiary Department now pays about 1500 Dollars, we have only been called upon to pay Eight Dollars for Assessments during that period, which would represent about $5.50 per Thousand Dollars. I think we may congratulate ourselves on the result of the year in this direction.

I must admit there has not been as rapid a growth as might reasonably be expected. This may be accounted for from the fact that we can only recruit our ranks from amongst the members of the A.O.U.W., many of whom do not deem it desirable to increase the amount of their Beneficiary. yet I think the connection with the A.O.U.W may account for our low death rate as we are selecting from selected men.

I must again appeal to the Beneficiary members of the Order to promptly meet their Assessments. Some Legions make their returns promptly, others are very careless. I have hesitated heretofore with regard to ordering the closing up of the Assessment on the day named in our constitution. Having now had two months in succession without Assessment, there cannot be any reasonable excuse for delay.

Some of the Grand Legions in the United States have decided to recommend separation from the A. O. U. W., at the first meeting of the Supreme Legion. At the meeting of our Grand Legion in May next the question will come up for action and I would therefore ask you to give careful thought to the matter so that your representative may be in a position to vote intelligently thereon, always bearing in mind that as the value of the Beneficiary Certificate increases, we must expect Assessments to increase in the same proportion.

I hope all Legions will remember that there is a social element in our Order as well as a Beneficiary one and make an effort to have the meetings regularly attended. This is requisite to keep up the interest in and the steady growth of the Order.

I am, Yours in E. I. &. U.,

W. J. PORTE, *Grand Commander.*

ATTEST : B. J. LEUBSDORF, *Grand Recorder.*

APPOINTMENTS.

I made the following appointments in addition to those mentioned in my circular of August 1st, 1888 :

P. Cdr. J. J. Ulley............for the Province of Quebec.
 " Henry Watson .... " Counties Elgin, Kent and Essex.
 " D. F. McWatt .... " North Simcoe, Muskoka and Parry Sound
 " C. Robson .... " Eastern Ontario.
 " W. R. Fenton......... " South Simcoe, North York and Peel.
P. Gd. Cdr. B. J. Leubsdorf .... " territory not otherwise occupied.
Cde. Geo. Lawrence........... " City of Winnipeg.

P. Cdr. Wyndow having resigned the position of D. D. G. C. for the County of York I filled the vacancy by appointing P. Cdr. Wm. J. Graham.

CONDITION OF THE ORDER.

From correspondence with several Legions, I find there is not as good an attendance at the regular meetings of the Legions as might reasonably be expected, and for reason already referred to our growth during the year has not been satisfactory.

Eglinton Legion No. 35 surrendered their charter, the members joined Toronto Legion No. 6.

Two new Legions were instituted since last session viz : Grenville No. 79, at Eastons Corners, by Deputy Grand Cdr. Robson, and Stanley No. 80, at Consecon, by D. D. Gd. Cdr. Spencer.

I learn from Grand Recorder that there were 202 certificates issued by him from May 1st, 1888 to date.

APPEALS.

There has not been a single case of appeal submitted to me. This of itself shows that harmony prevails in this jurisdiction.

DECISIONS.

1st.—In answer to a question proposed by the Grand Recorder June 25th. "The resolution passed by Grand Legion in regard to the examination of the urine speaks only about applicants for Beneficiary."

"How about parties who are over 45 years of age and are to be examined for reinstatement ?"

"Have they to be examined on this point also ?"

Ans.—The medical examination should be the same as the candidate had to pass at the time he obtained his Beneficiary Certificate.

This might seem to discriminate against those who may join after the 1st of August next. I do not look at it in that light, but rather what were the conditions on which a member joined the Order.

2nd.—I would not hold a Legion liable on per capita that was instituted less than a month before the 1st of January or the 1st of July.

3rd.—Should Grand Recorder answer questions as to state of Beneficiary? or, when certain Legions were suspended? and when reinstated? also to give names of Legions under suspension? and upon what assessments suspended?

Ans.—Each Legion has a right to know the standing of any Legion in the same jurisdiction. Therefore when such is asked for in regular form by any Legion they should have such information as would enable them to form an opinion of the value of the Beneficiary. This would not apply to enquiry made by individuals. A member of Picton Legion wrote to late Supreme Recorder Bohn, making enquiry concerning Supreme Beneficiary, he refused to give the explanation asked for unless made through the Recorder and bearing the seal of the Legion.

4th.—In answer to question "Is the sitting Commander not being a Past Commander eligible for election as representative to Grand Legion?

Yes—The custom in the A. O. U. W. is to recognize the retiring M. W. as eligible for representative and the Grand Legion of 1886 elected Commander J. McLean Stevenson then sitting Grand Commander as representative to Supreme Legion.

5th.—It is perfectly legal for the senior Past Commander present to install officers in the absence of D. D. G. C.

ASSSESSMENTS.

Assessments have not been remitted to the Grand Recorder by the proper Legion officers as promptly as our constitution and the best interests of the Order demand. The decision of Grand Legion of 1886 on document 15, pages 24 and 25 has prevented the carrying out of the 6th section, article 11, Grand Legion Constitution. I trust however that as soon as we are able to pay the maximum limit of 2000 Dollars on a death call, matters will come into a more settled state, because in that event the suspension of a few derelict Legions will not interfere with the full payment of the Beneficiary.

GRAND TREASURER.

Comrade R. G. Wright sent in his resignation as Grand Treasurer, which I did not at the time accept but as soon as I was satisfied his accounts were all right, I accepted it. In the meantime I had appointed Comrade J. McLean Stevenson to act in his stead.

I have found Grand Recorder B. J. Leubsdorf a most efficient officer and ready to give any information or aid necessary to the harmonious working of the Order ; and I would recommend the ordering of our finances so that as in the A.O.U. W. only one officer would require to give bonds to any large amount, and I would ask the Grand Legion to appoint a committee of five members, to arrange for such change as may be necessary to carry it into effect.

CONCLUSION.

In conclusion I desire to thank my Comrades for the uniform kindness I have received at their hands, and whenever I have failed to meet their expectations, I would assure them that in every case I did the best I could ; and in retiring from the position of Grand Commander (as I do not intend to be a candidate for re-election) I shall always consider myself indebted to my Comrades for their kind consideration, and I hope that my successor may receive their hearty support.

Fraternally submitted in E. I. & U.,

W. J. PORTE, *Grand Commander.*

PICTON, Ontario, April 1st, 1889.

REPORT

——OF THE——

GRAND TREASURER.

To the Grand Commander, Officers and Members of the Grand Legion, of Ontario, Select Knights.

COMRADES,—In the beginning of February last your Grand Commander did me the honor of appointing me to the office of Grand Treasurer, since which time I have received by remittance from the Grand Recorder on account of the several funds the following :

Beneficiary Funds $2997 00

Paid Warrant No. 24 Mrs. T. Holder 1461 00

Balance to Credit of Beneficiary Fund...$1536 00

General Fund...$ 982 18

Paid Warrants to amount of...................... 574 84

Balance to Credit of General Fund ......$ 407 34

All of which is respectfully submitted in E. I. & U.,

J. McL. STEVENSON, *Grand Treasurer.*

BARRIE, April 1st, 1889.

REPORT

—OF THE—

GRAND RECORDER.

——◦⟩◦⫸◂◦——

*To the Grand Commander, Officers and Members of the Grand
Legion of Ontario, Select Knights of the A. O. U. W.*

COMRADES :—I have the honor of submitting herewith in
detail the transactions of my office from May 1st, 1888 to date,
the day our fiscal year closes now in compliance with your
wishes as expressed at our last session.

During the last eleven months I collected in all $12034.52
an amount larger by $1318.89 than the total receipts of the
preceding 12 months.

On May 1st, 1888 our Grand Treasurer held to the credit
of the General Fund the sum of..........................$ 404 36.
Since that day and up to date I have collected and
paid over to him :

 a. For per Capita Tax $1672 00
 b. "   Beneficiary Certificates 208 00
 c. "   Supplies sold 291 67
 d. "   Charter Fees.................... 300 00
 e. "   the General Fund 86 85 $2558 52

    Total....................................... $2962 88

  Against which were drawn as per
Schedule A. 82 Warrants, aggregating ... $2555 54

leaving a balance of .... $ 407 34
to the credit of the General Fund at this day in the hands of
the Grand Treasurer after all Warrants drawn to date have
been paid.

  Schedule D. contains the details of all General Fund
collections.

The amount held by Grand Treasurer on May 1st, 1888 and belonging to the Beneficiary Fund was......$1831 00 my detailed statement Schedule G. shows that I collected

On Assessment No. 2 arrears	$	49 00	
" Disab. Ass't " 1 "		73 00	
" Assessment " 3 (half dollar Ass't)...		740 50	
" " " 4		1366 50	
" " " 5		1398 00	
" " " 6		1433 00	
" " " 7		1419 00	
" " " 8		1461 00	
" " " 1 (1889)		1536 00	9476 00
Total			$11307 00

which sum has been distributed as per details given in Schedule I. and entirely exhausting that fund after all Warrants drawn to date have been redeemed by the Grand Treasurer.

The Grand Legion has issued to date in all...1816 Cert. there were issued to May 1st, 1888 ....1614 "

showing an increase during the year of.................202 Cert. which were issued to 46 different Legions as per Schedule J. herewith submitted. It is however worthy of particular notice that more than half of the whole number (105) were issued to seven Legions only, and this in itself is sufficient evidence that the largest number of our Legions are suffering from individual inactivity, local circumstances, or from a fault in our system in recruiting for membership. Our death rate has been exceedingly low, 6 in an average membership in good standing in the Ben. Dep't of 1450, or $4.14 per thousand—still this seems to have been no inducement to our Brethren of the A. O.U.W. to join our ranks. Our Charter Fee is lower than that of any other fraternal society furnishing Life Insurance on the Mutual Assessment plan and doing business in this province, the initiation fee in our Legions has been puposely reduced to a mere bagatelle compared with the fees of competing societies, the uniform has been made optional in order to prevent any complaint as to expense in that direction, nevertheless all these means have failed, except in a very few notable instances, to infuse life into our Legions or to increase our membership by the addition of new Legions to our roll. Under these circumstances and especially if we remember that we this day already carry an obligation of over 2,500,000 Dollars, it behoves us as thinking men to take such steps as to place it beyond a doubt that we can meet that obligation promptly at such time as it may mature, preventing at the same time the financial demands upon our membership becoming too oppressive. Everyone acquainted with the history of fraternal societies and the conditions of the principles on which their existence is based, is aware of the necessity of *continuous* addition of new blood of proper physical qualification and of proper age in sufficient numbers, in order to reduce the average age and to keep down the assessments within a certain limit. The question now before us is: Are we, as an Order, doing what is necessary to comply with these conditions? In my opinion we are not and if you agree with me on this point, then the next step in order will be to select a remedy. To lay the matter on the table for another year, to take chances whether an improvement will come from itself without a change in our system, in other words to be afraid for some imaginary reason or other, to do now with good grace what we will be compelled to do a year hence as a matter of necessity, would in my opinion be most unwise. The remedy, easiest to accomplish and obviously the most suitable for the purpose, would be for you to say: We will permit good men of proper moral and physical qualification to join our ranks be they Workmen or not and any Legion of this jurisdiction existing this day may admit them to membership if it so chooses. Now consider for a moment what this simple act of legislation will accomplish: To-day we can only select our increase from a body of men, 14000 or thereabouts strong, the large majority of which carry all the insurance they can afford to pay for and the balance is to a great extent too old to join our Beneficiary Department. To-morrow our field of resources being enlarged by a simple vote of yours we find that we have the choice amongst at least 800,000 of proper individuals, who to the largest extent carry no insurance at all.

I have levied during the year 6 death Assessments viz:— Nos. 4. 5. 6. 7. 8. and 1. and Disability Assessment No. 2, the latter being paid by the Legions this month. For particulars as to collections made by me on each Assessment, I refer you to Schedule G.

I would also state that all death losses occurring in our membership up to date have been settled and thus we carry no obligation on this account over into the new fiscal year.

The policy adopted last year to send to each member a suspension notice direct from this office on receipt of official notification of suspension from the Legion of which he is a member, has been continued by me and has proved itself as one of the best means yet known, to prevent the loss of members. In a very large number of cases the Comrades received from me the first intimation of the suspension of their Beneficiary Certificates and as a rule they paid up immediately. I feel satisfied that we have lost more members through the negligence or lack of interest on the part of the Legion Officers than from any other cause.

You will notice from my statement showing the transactions in the Beneficiary Department, that our net increase during the year of Certificates in good standing was 179. There are this day 23 Certificates under temporary suspension.

In compliance with your wishes, as expressed at the session of 1888, I have taken pains to furnish the additional information then found wanting and I trust that my efforts in this direction will meet with your approval.

In my report last year I expressed the hope that we would have at the expiration of this fiscal year 2000 members in good standing in the Beneficiary Department. These hopes have not been realized, sorry to say, but I do not feel discouraged on that account. With an excellent membership, physically and morally speaking, coupled with a strict medical supervision from the very beginning of our Beneficiary Department, and last, but not least, with a death rate FAR BELOW THE AVERAGE, we are destined to become one of the leading fraternal and beneficial societies in this Province and in the Dominion, if you, in your wisdom, are willing to grant to your Legions and your Grand Officers that freedom of action that is necessary to accomplish the purpose.

In conclusion I beg to express my sincere thanks to you for the many courtesies and expressions of confidence extended to me.

Fraternally submitted in E. I. & U.,

B. J. Lewisdorf - G. R.

St. Catharines, April 1st, 1889.

Statement of Warrants drawn on the Grand Treasurer against the General Fund.

No.	IN WHOSE FAVOR	TO PAY	AMOUNT.
227	B. J. Leubsdorf, G. R..........	Expenses of Bond..........	$ 7 50
228	" "	Salary to May 17th, 1888. ..	72 00
229	" "	Postal Cards, Ass. 4........	14 80
230	C. Robson, Dep. Gd. Cdr.......	Institution Fee, No. 75	25 00
231	John Curran...................	Official Page to June 1, 1888.	25 00
232	W. R. Fenton, D. G. C.	Institution Fee, No. 76	25 00
233	B. J. Leubsdorf, G. R	Postage,trav.exp.&c. May '88	22 50
234	W. R. Fenton. D. G. C.	Institution Fee, No. 77, ...	25 00
235	Henry Watson, D. G. C........	" " " 78, ...	25 00
236	Brown Brothers	Stationery	12 58
237	R. G. Wright, G. T.	Allowance voted him '......	100 00
238	" "	Postage & Exchange, 1887 ..	3 83
239	Joseph Harton, ...	Services Journal Clerk......	10 00
240	Hy. M. Wilkinson.............	Printing	4 50
241	Chas. Logan.................	Furniture hire	2 00
242	Mrs. E. McGuire	Cleaning Lodge Room	1 00
243	R. G. Wright, G. T............	Pay Roll Session, 1888......	522 27
244	E. Bryson....................	Post Cards, Ass. No. 5	15 00
245	B. J. Leubsdorf, G. R..........	Postage Office exps. June. '88	17 55
246	Lockwood & Ough	One Copy book	2 25
247	R. Lawrie	P. O. Box pro. 1888	2 00
248	John Paul	Signmanual G. Cmdr.......	2 25
249	James Watt	Attendance Fin. Com	2 00
250	George Woltz.................	" "	2 00
251	Jos. Harton	" "	2 00
252	B. J. Leubsdorf, G. R..........	" "	6 32
253	R. G. Wright, G. T	Exp's Bond, Gd. Treas.	12 50
254	E. Bryson	Post Cards Ass. No. 6.......	15 00
255	R. C. Hill, Supr. Rdr..........	Acct. per Capita Tax	100 00
256	C. Robson. D. G. C...........	Institution Fee, No. 79......	25 00
257	B. J. Leubsdorf, G. R..........	Postage Tel. act., July 1888.	17 35
258	John S. King, G. M. E........	Fee for Exam and Postage..	29 68
259	B.J. Leubsdorf, G. R..........	Account of Salary..........	125 00
260	Henry M. Wilkinson	Printing	21 75
261	E. Bryson	Post Cards for Ass. No. 7 ..	15 00
262	R. C. Hill, S. Rdr.............	Account P. C. Tax	100 00
263	B. J. Leubsdorf, G. R.	Postage, Office exp. Aug. '88.	17 20
264	E. Bryson	Post Cards Ass. No. 8	15 15
265	C. Sherwood	Printing	133 10
266	B. J. Leubsdorf. G. R..........	Postage, Office exp. Sept. '88.	15 05
267	George Tait & Co.	Stationery	33 25
268	James Watt	Attendance Fin. Com	2 00
269	B. J. Leubsdorf G. R..........	" "	6 32
270	Geo. Woltz	" "	2 00
271	F. C. Spencer, D. G. C.	Institution Fee No. 80......	25 00
272	B. J. Leubsdorf, G. R..........	Postage, Office exp., Oct. 88.	14 50
273	" "	Account of Salary..........	125 00
274	D. D'E. Potter...............	Insurance on Supplies......	2 00
275	B. J Leubsdorf, G. R. ....,	Postage, Office exp. Nov, '88.	12 95
276	W. C. Richardson, S. R.	Balance P. C. Tax	100 20
277	" "	Supplies	3 10
278	E. Bryson	Post Cards Ass. No. 1	15 75
279	B. J. Leubsdorf, G. R..........	Postage, Office exp. Dec. '88.	11 65
280	Hy. M. Wilkinson	Printing	47 50
281	" "	Grant Can. Overseer	25 00
282	John S. King, G. M. E........	Examination Fee and Postg'e	18 04

283	James Watt	Attendance Fin. Com	2	00
284	George Woltz	" "	2	00
285	Jos. Harton	" "	2	00
286	B. J. Leubsdorf, G. R.	" "	6	32
287	N. Morey	Carp't work and mov. offnice.	20	00
288	Cooke & Son	Timber for office	6	57
289	B. J. Leubsdorf G. R	Postage, office exp , Jan. 89.	15	35
290	" "	Account of Salary	125	00
291	Hy. Watson, D. G. C	Reviving Marine No. 74	9	20
292	B. J. Leubsdorf, G. R	Postage, office exp., Feb. '89	12	45
293	Hy. M. Wilkinson	Grant Overs. and Printing	32	75
294	E. Bryson	Post Cards D. Ass, No. 2	16	29
295	B. J. Leubsdorf, G. R	Postage, office exp. March '89	14	85
296	C. Sherwood	Printing	33	50
297	B. J. Leubsdorf, G. R.	Salary to April 1st, '89	125	00
298	John S. King, M. D.	Examination Fee and Postage	19	57
299	James Watt	Postage for the year	4	00
300	Wm. J. Porte, G. C.	" and Telegraphing	7	43
301	R. G. Wright	Salary as G. T. 9 months	37	50
302	R. W. Osborn	Bookbinding	7	56
303	R. G. Wright	Postage and Exp's as G. T,	2	28
304	John Sutter	Coal for Gd. R's office	6	25
305	James Watt	Attendance Fin. Com	2	00
306	Joseph Harton	" "	2	00
307	George Woltz	" "	2	00
308	B. J. Leubsdorf, G. R.	" "	6	32
			2555	54

SCHEDULE B. Expense Account of the Grand Legion.

Paid for Expenses of Session 1888, including Journal Clerk ....$ 535 27
" " Grant Canadian Overseer................................. 43 75
" " Expressage, Telegraph, Duty, Postage, Office Expenses, &c .. 193 19
" " Fixing Grand Recorder's Office and for moving.............. 26 57
" " Coal and Light " " 6 25
" " Grand Recorder's Salary including arrears from last term 572 00
" " Meetings Finance Committee............................. 47 28
" " Grand Medical Examiner's Fees and expenses 67 29
" " Institution Fees 6 Legions 150 00
" " Reviving weak Legions.................................... 9 20
" " Printing and Binding Free Supplies and Stationery.......... 126 28
" " Insurance and Supplies 2 00
" " Premium on Officers Bonds............................... 20 00
" " Supreme Legion P. C. Tax 300 20
" " Grant Grand Treasurer 100 00
" " Salary Grand Treasurer 37 50
" " Stereotyping Quarterly Reports........................... 5 25
" " Grant Canadian Workman 25 00

$2267 03

SCHEDULE C.—Statement showing the number of Beneficiary Certificates issued for the six fiscal years from May 24th, 1883, to April 1st, 1889.

Issued during fiscal year 1883-84 ....287 Certificates.
" " " " 1884-85 ....310 "
" " " " 1885-86 ....404 "
" " " " 1886-87 ....302 "
" " " " 1887-88 ....311 "
" " " " 1888-89 ....202 "

Total issued to April 1st, 1889................ 1816 Certificates.
Average per year 302 Certificates.

Statement of moneys received for the General Fund from May 1st, 1888, to April 1st, 1889.

Legion.	No.	P. C. Tax.	Supplies.	Ben. Cer.	Charter.	Gl. Fund
Lincoln	1	$ 39 50	$ 6 41	$	$	$ .. ..
Niagara Falls..	2	15 00	1 21	1 00	....	.. ..
Wentworth	3	38 00	3 21	2 00	....	.. 50
Union	4	.. ..	.. ..	.. ..	....	.. ..
Star	5	11 50	.. 85	1 00	....	.. 50
Toronto	6	121 00	21 09	1 00	....	.. ..
Parkdale	7	11 00	76	2 00	....	.. ..
Seguin	8	8 00	3 84	.. ..	....	.. ..
Bradford	9	24 00	6 24	.. ..	....	.. ..
Kingston	10	40 50	10 69	5 00	....	.. 50
Lynden	11	12 00	2 06	.. ..	....	.. ..
Iroquois	12	11 00	.. ..	.. ..	....	.. ..
Jarvis	13	.. ..	.. ..	.. ..	....	.. ..
Picton	14	49 50	8 44	.. ..	....	.. 50
Caledonia	15	15 00	.. ..	1 00	....	.. ..
Kempenfeldt ..	16	38 00	2 98	3 00	....	.. ..
Frontier	17	7 00	.. 05	.. ..	....	.. ..
Guelph	18	30 50	2 64	2 00	....	.. 50
Tilsonburg	19	6 00	1 43	.. ..	....	.. ..
Erin	20	12 50	4 39	.. ..	....	.. 50
Excelsior	21	22 00	23 29	1 00	....	.. ..
Phœnix	22	10 00	.. 90	.. ..	....	.. ..
York	23	45 00	16 20	4 00	....	.. 50
Lennox	24	28 00	2 83	1 00	....	.. ..
Equity	25	11 00	.. ..	.. ..	....	.. ..
Leopold	26	38 00	1 75	2 00	....	.. 50
Victoria	27	9 50	3 06	1 00	....	.. ..
Fergus	28	.. ..	.. ..	.. ..	....	.. ..
Fenton	29	15 50	2 80	1 00	....	.. ..
Shelburne	30	21 50	2 65	1 00	....	.. ..
Morrisburg ..	31	16 50	.. ..	.. ..	....	.. ..
Island	32	20 50	.. ..	1 00	....	.. ..
Capital	33	31 50	12 82	9 00	....	.. ..
Orillia	34	15 50	5 88	.. ..	....	.. ..
Eglinton	35	.. ..	6 83	.. ..	....	.. ..
Whitby	36	19 50	.. 99	1 00	....	.. 50
Stanhoff	37	7 00	2 00	.. ..	....	.. ..
Dufferin	38	55 50	4 86	4 ..	....	.. ..
Kemptville	39	17 50	1 32	.. ..	....	.. 50
Gordon	40	17 00	4 42	1 00	....	.. ..
Muskoka	41	7 00	1 26	2 00	....	.. 50
Collingwood ..	42	37 00	8 52	.. ..	....	.. ..
Durham	43	13 00	2 11	3 00	....	.. ..
Empress	44	20 00	1 26	.. ..	....	.. ..
Waterloo	45	9 00	.. ..	.. ..	....	.. ..
Mystic	46	41 50	7 65	3 00	....	.. ..
Lyn	47	20 00	4 46	5 00	....	.. ..
Rideau	48	15 00	1 71	.. ..	....	.. ..
Ontario	49	5 50	.. 63	.. ..	....	.. ..
Jamieson	50	12 50	4 26	.. ..	....	.. 50
Simcoe	51	18 00	1 62	.. ..	....	.. 50
Queen City ..	52	39 50	4 42	5 00	....	.. ..
Crystal	53	44 00	8 78	3 00	....	.. ..
Tottenham ..	54	16 50	.. ..	2 00	....	.. ..
Tamworth	55	20 00	1 71	.. ..	....	.. 50
Centreville	56	.. ..	.. ..	.. ..	....	.. ..

Name	Col1	Col2	Col3	Col4	Col5
Queensville ..57..............	15 00	3 94	4 00	....	.. ..
Royal ....58..............	12 50	5 35	.. ..	....	.. ..
Norfolk ......59..............	21 50	1 89	3 00	....	2 00
Morpeth......60..............	13 00	1 26	.. ..	....	.. ..
Howard ......61..............	16 25	5 49	.. ..	....	.. ..
Banner ......62..............	54 50	6 14	6 00	....	.. ..
Elmvale......63..............	19 50	4 21	1 00	....	.. 50
Belleville ....64..............	14 60	2 24	1 00	....	.. ..
Lake ....65..............	36 50	1 31	4 00	....	.. ..
Dunn ....66..............	12 50	1 00	4 00	....	.. 50
Dundas .....67..............	18 50	8 04	5 00	....	1 00
Hickcox .....68..............	39 00	2 60	.. ..	....	.. 50
Niagara .....69..............	23 50	8 58	2 00	....	.. ..
Brampton ....70..............	15 00	.. ..	.. ..	....	.. ..
Fidelity ......71..............	10 50	1 18	1 00	....	.. ..
Hillsburg ....72..............	7 50	1 58	.. ..	....	.. ..
Lorne ....73..............	12 00	1 00	1 00	....	.. ..
Marine ......74..............	6 50	2 25	5 00	....	.. ..
Lisgar........75..............	12 50	.. ..	15 00	50 00	.. 50
Caledon ......76..............	.. ..	.. ..	3 00	50 00	.. ..
Schomberg ..77..............	.. ..	.. ..	12 00	50 00	.. ..
Kingsville ....78..............	20 00	.. ..	25 00	50 00	.. ..
Grenville ....79..............	5 00	.. ..	9 00	50 00	.. ..
Stanley ......80..............	4 75	.. ..	3 00	50 00	.. ..
Pioneer, Q.... 1..............	21 50	9 00	10 00	....	.. ..
Stadacona, Q.. 2..............	44 50	5 83	26 00	....	2 50
Robert Pink	1 00	.. ..	.. ..	....	.. ..
H. F. Falkiner	1 00	.. ..	.. ..	....	.. ..
Wm. Tolmie	1 00	.. ..	.. ..	....	.. ..
T. P. Worth	1 00	.. ..	.. ..	....	.. ..
R. Doherty	1 00	.. ..	.. ..	....	.. ..
A. O. Andrews	.. 50	.. ..	.. ..	....	.. ..
B. F. Morley.................	1 00	.. ..	.. ..	....	.. ..
Jos. Harton	.. ..	1 25	.. ..	....	.. ..
Interest from G. Treasurer......	.. ..	.. ..	.. ..	....	72 35
	1672 00	291 67	208 00	300 00	86 85

SCHEDULE E.—Statement showing the transactions of the Beneficiary Department for the six fiscal years from May 24th, 1883, to April 1st, 1889.

Collected during fiscal year 1883-84.............................$ 203.00
" " " " 1884-85................................. 387 00
" " " " 1885-86................................. 737 00
" " " " 1886-87................................. 8808 00
" " " " 1887-88................................. 8293 00
" " " " 1888-89................................. 9476 00

$27904 00

Less paid out for the redemption of 25 Beneficiary Certificates $27904 00

Balance on hand ....$ 0000 00

SCHEDULE F.—Itemized Statement of Office Furniture on hand.

1 Safe $110 00
3 Files... 3 00
2 Files... 1 00
1 Letterpress....................................... 5 00
1 Scale... 1 00
1 Trunk 2 00
1 Tinbox... 2 00
1 Seal-electro...................................... 75
1 Office desk 19 20

$143 95

SCHEDULE G.

Statement of Beneficiary Fund collected from May 1st, 1888, to April 1st, 1889.

Legion.	No.	Ass. 2 $....	D.A. No 1 $.	Ass. 3 $15 00	Ass. 4 $30 00	Ass. 5 $30 00	Ass. 6 $30 00	Ass. 7 $30 00	Ass. 8 $30 00	Ass. i $29 00
Lincoln	1			6 ..	12 ..	12 ..	12 ..	12 ..	12 ..	13 ..
Niagara Falls	2			20 ..	34 ..	33 ..	33 ..	34 ..	34 ..	34 ..
Wentworth	3				1 ..	1 ..	1 ..	1 ..	1 ..	
Union	4			.50	7 ..	7 ..	7 ..	7 ..	7 ..	8 ..
Star	5			3 50	99 ..	109 ..	100 ..	111 ..	106 ..	113 ..
Toronto	6			49 50						9 ..
Parkdale	7		4 50	4 50	9 ..	9 ..	9 ..	10 ..	8 ..	8 ..
Seguin	8			4 ..	8 ..	8 ..	8 ..	8 ..		
Bradford	9			12 ..	24 ..	24 ..	24 ..	23 ..	23 ..	23 ..
Kingston	10		6 50	19 ..	37 ..	40 ..	40 ..	40 ..	40 ..	41 ..
Lynden	11	14 ..		6 50	11 ..	10 ..	11 ..	13 ..	10 ..	12 ..
Iroquois	12		3 50	3 ..	6 ..	6 ..	6 ..	6 ..	6 ..	6 ..
Jarvis	13									
Picton	14	7 ..		18 50	37 ..	36 ..	40 ..	37 ..	36 ..	38 ..
Caledonia	15		8 ..	15 50			28 ..	8 ..	19 50	10 ..
Kempenfeldt	16			.50	31 ..	31 ..	31 ..	31 ..	31 ..	32 ..
Frontier	17			13 ..	1 ..	1 ..	1 ..	1 ..	1 ..	1 ..
Guelph	18			3 50	28 ..	28 ..	29 ..	30 ..	31 ..	31 ..
Tilsonburg	19			5 50	6 ..	6 ..	6 ..	6 ..	6 ..	6 ..
Erin	20			11 ..	11 ..	9 ..	9 ..	12 ..	10 ..	
Excelsior	21			5 ..	22 ..	22 ..	20 ..	23 ..	24 ..	21 ..
Phœnix	22			23 ..	10 ..	10 ..	10 ..	10 ..	10 ..	10 ..
York	23			14 ..	37 ..	40 ..	38 ..	34 ..	35 ..	48 ..
Lennox	24			5 50	28 ..	28 ..	27 ..	29 ..	27 ..	29 ..
Equity	25			17 ..	11 ..	11 ..	11 ..	11 ..	11 ..	11 ..
Leopold	26			4 ..	24 ..	28 ..	32 ..	32 ..	34 ..	30 ..
Victoria	27				8 ..	8 ..	8 ..	8 ..	8 ..	9 ..
Fergus	28			8 ..						
Fenton	29		20 ..	10 ..	15 ..	16 ..	15 ..	10 ..	20 ..	15 ..
Shelburne	30			7 50	19 50	17 ..	19 ..	20 ..	23 ..	22 ..
Morrisburg	31			9 ..	15 ..	23 ..	15 ..	16 ..	16 ..	16 ..
Island	32				15 ..	15 ..	16 ..	16 ..	16 ..	16 ..

[17]

Legion	No.	Ass. 2	D.A. No. 1	Ass. 3	Ass. 4	Ass. 5	Ass. 6	Ass. 7	Ass. 8	Ass. 1
Capital	33			9	18	18	18	19	18	22
Orillia	34	28	7	8	17	17	17	17	17	19
Eglinton	35			5 50	11	11	11	11	11	12
Whitby	36			5 50	15	11	11	11	10	12
Stanhoff	37			7 50	15	15	15	14	14	10
Dufferin	38			25 50	52	52	52	53	53	53
Kemptville	39			7 50	15	15	15	15	15	15
Gordon	40			8	16	17	17	17	17	17
Muskoka	41		6 00	6	12	12	32	13	11	15
Collingwood	42			17 50	37	37	37	37	37	37
Durham	43			5 50	11	11	11	11	11	11
Empress	44			7	14	14	14	14	14	14
Waterloo	45			5	9	9	9	7	9	8
Mystic	46			19 50	37	42	39	40	41	41
Lyn	47		7 50	5 50	11	11	11	12	12	15
Rideau	48		3 50	7 50	15	15	15	15	15	15
Ontario	49			3 50	7	7	7	7	7	7
Jamieson	50			10	13	12	11	13	12	12
Simcoe	51			9	18	18	17	17	17	21
Queen City	52			18 50	34	36	35	37	37	38
Crystal	53			21 50	38	42	41	43	43	42
Tottenham	54			7	14	14	16	16	15	17
Tamworth	55			13	19	30	16	22	23	20
Centreville	56									
Queensville	57			4 50	9	9	9	9	9	9
Royal	58			6	12	12	12	12	11	11
Norfolk	59			10	21	21	20	20	21	21
Morpeth	60		6 50	9	12	15	16	11	15	15
Howard	61			6 50	13	13	13	13	13	13
Banner	62			14 50	24	23	23	23	21	23
Elmvale	63			7 50	19	16	16	16	16	16

	$1536 00	$1461 00	$1419 00	$1433 00	$1398 00	$1366 50	$740 50	$73 00	$49 00
Belleville 64	13	13	13	13	13	12	6 00		
Lake 65	10	9	9	9	9	9	4 50		
Dunn 66	13	15 50	10	9	9	9	7 50		
Dundas 67	18	16	15	14	15	16	8		
Hickcox 68	39	39	39	39	39	39	19 50		
Niagara 69	23	23	23	24	24	24	12		
Brampton 70	15	15	15	15	15	15	7 50		
Fidelity 71	10	10	10	10	10	10	5		
Hillsburg ...72	15	15	15	15	15	15	7 50		
Lorne 73	12	12	11	11	11	11	11		
Marine 74	19	12	13	18	9	11	11		
Lisgar 75	15	11							
Caledon 76	1	2		1	1				
Schomberg ...77									
Kingsville ..78	24	15							
Grenville ...79	9								
Stanley 80	1								
Pioneer, Q. 1	25	18	17	17	17	17	14		
Stadacona, Q. 2	49	41	40	33	33	23	21		
Robert Pink	1	1	1	1	1	1	50		
H. F. Falkiner	1	1	1		1	1	50		
Wm. Tolmie	1	1	2		1	1	50		
T. P. Worth	1	1	1	1	1	1	50		
R. Doherty	1	1	1	1	1	1	50		
A. O. Andrews									
B. F. Morley	1								

SCHEDULE H.

Statement of Beneficiary Certificate issued to each Legion in the jurisdiction from May 1st, 1888, to April 1st, 1889.

No.	Name of Legion.	No. of Certificat's	No.	Name of Legion.	No. of Certificat's
1	Lincoln	None..	42	Collingwood	None..
2	Niagara Falls	1	43	Durham	3
3	Wentworth	2	44	Empress	None..
4	Union	None..	45	Waterloo	None..
5	Star	1	46	Mystic	3
6	Toronto	1	47	Lyn	5
7	Cooksville	2	48	Rideau	None..
8	Seguin	None..	49	Ontario	None..
9	Bradford	None..	50	Jamieson	None..
10	Kingston	5	51	Simcoe	None..
11	Lynden	None..	52	Queen City	6
12	Iroquois	None..	53	Crystal	3
13	Jarvis	None..	54	Tottenham	4
14	Picton	None..	55	Tamworth	None..
15	Caledonia	1	56	Centreville	None..
16	Kempenfeldt	3	57	Queensville	4
17	Frontier	None.	58	Royal	None..
18	Wellington	2	59	Norfolk	3
19	Tilsonburg	None..	60	Morpeth	None..
20	Erin	None	61	Howard	None..
21	Excelsior	1	62	Banner	2
22	Phœnix	None..	63	Elmvale	1
23	York	4	64	Belleville	1
24	Lennox	None..	65	Lake	4
25	Equity	None..	66	Dunn	4
26	Leopold	2	67	Dundas	5
27	Victoria	1	68	Hickcox	None..
28	Fergus	None..	69	Niagara	None..
29	Fenton	1	70	Brampton	None..
30	Shelburne	1	71	Fidelity	1
31	Morrisburg	None..	72	Hillsburg	None.,
32	Island	1	73	Lorne	1
33	Capital	9	74	Marine	4
34	Orillia	None..	75	Lisgar	15
35	Eglinton	None..	76	Caledon	3
36	Whitby	1	77	Schomberg	12
37	Stanhoff	None..	78	Kingsville	25
38	Dufferin	4	79	Grenville	9
39	Kemptville	None..	80	Stanley	3
40	Gordon	1	1	Pioneer, Q	10
41	Muskoka	2	2	Stadacona, Q	25

SCHEDULE I.—Statement of Warrants drawn upon the Grand Treasurer against the Beneficiary Fund.

No. 18 in favor of Mrs. Mary Ann Jenkins	$ 1289 00
" 19 " " " Hattie Little	1404 50
" 20 " " " Amelia M. Brouse	1366 50
" 21 " " " Sarah Jane Strachan	699 00
" 21½ " " Miss Ada Strachan	699 00
" 22 " " Mrs. Elizabeth McDonald	1433 00
" 23 " " " Mary Ann Reid	1419 00
" 24 " " " Elizabeth Holder	1461 00
" 25 " " " Elizabeth A. Barnes	1536 00

$11307 00

SCHEDULE J.

List of Beneficiary Certificates Annulled from May 1st, 1888 to March 31st, 1889 inclusive.

No. Cer.	Name.	Legion.	No.	Date Annulling Certificate
38	Ramsay, W. J.	Toronto	6	February 1st, 1889.
470	Endean, John	"	6	" 1st, 1889.
608	Downey, Thomas	"	6	" 1st, 1889.
1271	Harrison, Wm. S.	Cooksville	7	" 1st, 1889.
1022	Harper, Robert	Bradford	9	March 1st, 1889.
332	Weaver, Joseph	Lynden	11	January 1st, 1889.
1356	Markle, Jac. Hiram	"	11	February 1st, 1889.
90	Hoshal, John A.	Iroquois	12	January 1st, 1889.
261	Atkinson, John S.	Picton	14	February 1st, 1889.
173	Smuck, Osborne	Caledonia	15	July 1st, 1888.
211	Watson, John H.	Kempenfeldt	16	September 1st, 1888.
351	Saunders, Henry P	"	16	" 1st, 1888.
820	Glass, Samuel F.	Tilsonburg	19	June 1st, 1888.
1190	Dixon, Richard F.	"	19	December 1st, 1888.
629	Justice, Adam	Erin	20	September 1st, 1888
193	Bills, Thos. Henry	Excelsior	21	July 1st, 1888.
247	Quinn, Robert	"	21	April 1st, 1889.
257	Saunders, A. E.	York	23	March 1st, 1889.
259	Delaporte, Alexander	"	23	January 1st, 1889.
285	Laker, Chas. W	"	23	January 1st, 1889.
294	Harris, James	"	23	" 1st, 1889.
296	Coulter, John	"	23	December 1st, 1888.
437	Sheriff, John G.	"	23	March 1st, 1889.
612	Pitts, James E	"	23	January 1st, 1889.
673	MacDonald, Archibald	"	23	February 1st 1889.
699	Lawrence, Geo	"	23	September 1st, 1888.
797	Banfield, Wm. S.	"	23	March 1st, 1889.
375	Calhoun, Alfred J	Shelburne	30	January 1st, 1889.
1276	McCutcheon, Wm	"	30	November 1st, 1888.
463	Mott, John Jacob	Stanhoff	37	December 1st, 1888.
668	Cunningham James	Waterloo	45	April 1st, 1889.
843	Haffner, Frederick	Jamieson	50	June 1st, 1888.
755	Wilson Samuel	"	50	January 1st, 1889.
759	Usher, John A	"	50	August 1st, 1888.
822	King, Andrew	"	50	" 1st, 1888.
1460	Wood, William	"	50	December 1st, 1888.
301	Saniger, Wm. P.	Queen City	52	June 1st, 1888.
359	Chapman, Thomas	Crystal	53	August 1st, 1888.
1123	Clarke, W. F.	"	53	June 1st, 1888.
1202	Bishop, Albert	Elmvale	63	September 1st. 1888.
1213	Bishop, George	"	63	" 1st. 1888.
1366	Foster, James	Dunn	66	July 1st, 1888.
1371	Bush, Jonas T.	"	66	" 1st, 1888.
1287	Cormack, Magness	Dundas	67	February 1st. 1888.
1289	Morin, Jacques	"	67	January 1st, 1889.
1330	Scarlett, William	Hickcox	68	September 1st, 1888.
1320	Murray, William	Niagara	69	April 1st, 1889.
1536	Leggatt, John Hy. C.	Marine	74	February 1st, 1889.
1540	Tomlinson, Jos. W	"	74	" 1st, 1889.
1587	Fox, Albert	"	74	April 1st, 1889.
1597	Maloney, Fred J	"	74	February 1st, 1889.
1419	McMichael, Franklin J	Mystic	46	Cancl'd Dec. 11' 88

Annulled Certificates re-instated during the year.

485.. Henderson, Edward, Shelburne 30.
675.. McKinney, Alexander, Shelburne 30.
426.. Chamberlain, Thos. F., Morrisburg 31.

SCHEDULE K.

Statement showing the members in good standing on March 31st, 1889.

No.	Name of Legion.	No. of Members.	No.	Name of Legion.	No. of Members.
1	Lincoln	39	42	Collingwood	37
2	Niagara Falls	15	43	Durham	14
3	Wentworth	37	44	Empress	20
4	Union		45	Waterloo	8
5	Star	12	46	Mystic	42
6	Toronto	119	47	Lyn	18
7	Cooksville	9	48	Rideau	15
8	Seguin	8	49	Ontario	8
9	Bradford	24	50	Jamieson	10
10	Kingston	42	51	Simcoe	18
11	Lynden	11	52	Queen City	41
12	Iroquois	6	53	Crystal	50
13	Jarvis		54	Tottenham	16
14	Picton	49	55	Tamworth	20
15	Caledonia	11	56	Centreville	
16	Kempenfeldt	39	57	Queensville	16
17	Frontier	7	58	Royal	12
18	Wellington	31	59	Norfolk	23
19	Tilsonburg	6	60	Morpeth	13
20	Erin	11	61	Howard	13
21	Excelsior	21	62	Banner	29
22	Phœnix	10	63	Elmvale	21
23	York	43	64	Belleville	14
24	Lennox	27	65	Lake	37
25	Equity	11	66	Dunn	14
26	Leopold	41	67	Dundas	18
27	Victoria	10	68	Hickcox	39
28	Fergus		69	Niagara	23
29	Fenton	15	70	Brampton	15
30	Shelburne	22	71	Fidelity	11
31	Morrisburg	16	72	Hillsburg	15
32	Island	20	73	Lorne	12
33	Capital	36	74	Marine	15
34	Orillia	18	75	Lisgar	17
35	Eglinton		76	Caledon	4
36	Whitby	20	77	Schomberg	12
37	Stanhoff	11	78	Kingsville	24
38	Dufferin	55	79	Grenville	11
39	Kemptville	17	80	Stanley	19
40	Gordon	17	1	Pioneer, Q	27
41	Muskoka	13	2	Stadacona, Q	55

Under charge of Grand Recorder 6.

Total............ 1731

SCHEDULE L.

List of Legions instituted since my last report.

Name of Legion.	No.	Location.	By whom instituted.	Date of Institution
Kingsville	78	Kingsville	D. G. C. Watson	June 8th, 1888
Grenville	79	Eastons Corn.	D. G. C. Robson	July 23rd, 1888.
Stanley	80	Consecon	D. D. G. C. Spencer	October 1st, 1888.

Statement showing the transactions in the Beneficiary Department from May 1st, 1888 to April 1st, 1889.

Legion.	No.	Good Standing May 1,'89.	Cert. Iss'd	Re-instated	Joined by Card.	Suspended.	Annulled.	Died.	Withdrawn	In force Apl 1,'89
Lincoln	1	30	..	..	..	1	..	..	..	29
Niagara Falls	2	12	1	..	..	..	..	..	..	13
Wentworth	3	35	2	..	..	..	..	2	..	35
Union	4	1	..	..	..	..	..	..	1	..
Star	5	7	1	..	..	..	..	..	..	8
Toronto	6	99	1	..	11	1	3	..	..	107
Parkdale	7	9	2	..	..	1	1	..	..	9
Seguin	8	8	..	..	..	..	..	..	..	8
Bradford	9	24	..	..	..	1	1	..	..	22
Kingston	10	38	5	..	..	..	..	1	..	42
Lynden	11	13	..	..	..	..	2	..	..	11
Iroquois	12	7	..	..	..	..	1	..	..	6
Jarvis	13	..	..	..	..	..	..	..	..	..
Picton	14	38	..	..	..	..	1	..	..	37
Caledonia	15	7	1	3	..	..	..	..	..	11
Kempenfeldt	16	30	3	..	1	..	..	..	..	34
Frontier	17	1	..	..	..	..	..	..	..	1
Guelph	18	28	2	..	1	..	..	..	..	31
Tilsonburg	19	7	..	..	..	..	1	..	..	6
Erin	20	11	..	..	..	1	..	..	1	9
Excelsior	21	22	1	..	..	1	1	..	..	21
Phœnix	22	10	..	..	..	..	..	..	..	10
York	23	47	4	..	..	..	9	1	..	41
Lennox	24	28	..	..	..	1	..	..	..	27
Equity	25	11	..	..	..	..	..	..	..	11
Leopold	26	29	2	1	..	..	..	..	..	32
Victoria	27	8	1	..	..	..	..	..	..	9
Fergus	28	..	..	..	..	..	..	..	..	..
Fenton	29	14	2	1	..	..	..	..	1	16
Shelburne	30	16	1	5	..	1	1	..	..	20
Morrisburg	31	15	..	1	..	..	..	..	..	16
Island	32	16	1	..	..	..	..	..	1	16
Capital	33	18	9	..	..	..	..	..	..	27
Orillia	34	..	..	17	1	..	..	..	..	18
Eglinton	35	11	..	..	..	..	..	..	11	..
Whitby	36	11	1	..	..	..	..	..	..	12
Stanhoff	37	16	..	..	..	4	1	..	..	11
Dufferin	38	52	4	..	..	2	..	..	..	54
Kemptville	39	15	..	..	..	..	..	..	..	15
Gordon	40	17	1	..	..	..	..	..	1	17
Muskoka	41	12	2	..	..	1	..	..	..	13
Collingwood	42	37	..	..	..	..	..	..	..	37
Durham	43	11	3	..	..	..	..	..	..	14
Empress	44	14	..	..	..	..	..	..	..	14
Waterloo	45	8	..	..	..	..	..	..	..	8
Mystic	46	39	3	..	..	..	1	..	..	41
Lyn	47	11	5	..	..	..	..	..	..	16
Rideau	48	15	..	..	..	..	..	..	..	15
Ontario	49	7	..	..	..	..	..	..	..	7
Jamieson	50	12	..	1	..	..	1	..	..	12
Simcoe	51	18	..	..	..	..	..	..	..	18
Queen City	52	32	6	3	..	2	..	..	..	39
Crystal	53	42	3	..	..	2	..	..	..	43
Tottenham	54	14	4	..	..	1	..	..	..	17
Tamworth	55	18	..	2	..	..	..	..	..	20

Centreville....56....	..	..	..	..	..	..	..	..	..
Queensville ..57....	9	4	..	..	..	..	..	..	13
Royal ....58....	12	..	..	..	..	..	..	1	11
Norfolk ......59....	21	3	..	..	..	1	..	..	23
Morpeth......60....	13	..	..	..	:	..	..	..	13
Howard ......61....	13	..	..	..	..	..	..	..	13
Banner ......62....	24	2	..	..	2	..	1	..	23
Elmvale ......63....	15	1	1	..	..	..	..	..	17
Belleville ....64....	12	1	..	..	..	..	..	..	13
Lake ....65....	9	4	..	..	..	..	..	..	13
Dunn ....66....	9	4	1	..	..	..	..	..	14
Dundas ......67....	15	5	..	..	..	1	..	1	18
Hickcox ......68....	39	..	..	..	..	..	..	..	39
Niagara ......69....	24	..	..	..	..	1	..	..	23
Brampton ....70....	15	..	..	..	..	..	..	..	15
Fidelity ......71....	10	1	..	..	..	..	..	..	11
Hillsburg ....72....	15	..	..	..	..	..	..	..	15
Lorne ....73....	10	1	..	1	..	..	..	..	12
Marine ......74....	16	4	..	..	1	4	..	..	15
Lisgar........75....	..	15	..	1	..	..	..	..	16
Caledon ......76....	..	3	..	1	..	..	..	..	4
Schomberg ..77....	..	12	..	..	..	..	..	..	12
Kingsville ....78....	..	25	..	..	1	..	..	..	24
Grenville ....79....	..	9	..	..	..	..	..	..	9
Stanley ......80....	..	3	..	..	..	..	..	..	3
Pioneer, Q.... 1....	17	10	..	..	..	..	..	..	27
Stadacona, Q.. 2....	31	25	..	..	1	..	..	..	55
Under charge of G.R.	5	..	..	1	..	..	..	..	6
	1384	202	36	18	23	31	5	18	1563

RECAPITULATION

In good standing May 1st, 1888	1384
Certificates issued	202
Reinstated	36
Joined by Card..	18
	1640

FROM WHICH DEDUCT.

Suspended	23	
Annulled..	31	
Withdrawn	18	
Died..	5	77
Leaving in good standing..................		1563
Net increase during the year		179

SCHEDULE L.—Supplies Account.

DR.

To Stock on hand May 1st, 1888.....................................$	365	37
" Goods purchased from Supreme Legion.........................	3	10
" Paid for Printing Supplies...	172	75
" Paid for Binding Supplies...	5	71
" Paid for Postal Cards for Assessments	121	65
" Profit	115	07
	$783	65

CR.

By Supplies sold...$	261	64
" Supplies furnished free of charge................................	149	54
" Stock on hand April 1st, 1889	372	47
	$783	65

SCHEDULE O.

Statement of amounts due Grand Legion from Subordinate Legions.

Lincoln	1	$ 90	Lyn	47		47
Niagara Falls	2	1 39	Rideau	48	1	92
Wentworth	3	1 03	Ontario	49		83
Toronto	6	3 40	Jamieson	50		42
Cooksville	7	1 20	Simcoe	51		54
Seguin	8	96	Queen City	52	5	32
Bradford	9	72	Crystal	53	1	34
Kingston	10	1 33	Tottenham	54	2	83
Lynden	11	1 00	Tamworth	55		60
Iroquois	12	2 20	Queensville	57	4	29
Picton	14	1 20	Norfolk	59		65
Caledonia	15	2 05	Morpeth	60		42
Kempenfeldt	16	1 89	Howard	61	3	63
Wellington	18	96	Bannar	62	1	72
Tilsonburg	19	23	Elmvale	63		49
Excelsior	21	72	Belleville	64	1	39
Phoenix	22	30	Lake	65	1	19
York	23	3 50	Dunn	66	1	26
Lennox	24	3 36	Dundas	67		60
Equity	25	4 14	Hickcox	68	5	40
Leopold	26	3 67	Niagara	69	1	94
Fenton	29	1 92	Brampton	70	2	23
Shelburne	30	1 90	Fidelity	71		30
Morrisburg	31	2 89	Hillsburg	72		45
Island	32	2 50	Lorne	73		85
Capital	33	97	Marine	74		80
Orillia	34	54	Lisgar	75	6	58
Whitby	36	35	Caledon	76		03
Stanhoff	37	2 08	Schomberg	77		18
Dufferin	38	1 69	Kingsville	78		99
Kemptville	39	95	Grenville	79		27
Gordon	40	54	Stanley	80		07
Muskoka	41	1 50	Pioneer, Q.	1	1	78
Collingwood	42	1 14	Stadacona Q	2	1	59
Durham	43	1 38				
Empress	44	1 42				
Waterloo	45	1 88				
Mystic	46	1 20			$ 114	37

Amounts due Subordinate Legions.

Erin	20	$ 17	Fergus	28	$ 25
Victoria	27	1 73	Royal	58	67
					$2 82

SCHEDULE P.—Balance Sheet pro April 1st, 1889.

Dr.			Cr.	
To Erin Legion No. 20	$ 17		By Cash on hand	$ 407 34
" Victoria " " 27	1 73		" Office furniture	143 95
" Fergus " " 28	25		" Supplies in stock	372 47
" Royal " " 58	67		" Outstanding accounts	114 37
" Canadian Workman	12 50			
" " Overseer	12 50			$1038 13
" Balance	1010 31			
	$1038 13		By bal. in favor of Grand Legion	$1010 31

SCHEDULE Q.—Itemized Statement of Supplies on hand.

690..Application Cards ......$\frac{1}{2}$	3 45
72..Statement..............o1	72
..Med. Exam. Blanks	21 00
1..Digest	2 00
19..Drill books 85	16 50
32..Rituals 100	32 00
7..Treas. Receipt books....24	1 68
10..Rec. Treas. Rect. book..24	2 40
1..Warrant books...........	24
5..Supreme Constitutions..o6	30
12..Benfy. Ret. books 24	2 76
27..Withdrawal Cards......o5	1 35
4..Roll books 35	1 40
11..Monthly Report books ..45	4 95
11..Beneficiary Registers..,..45	4 95
120..Journals Session 1885 ..15	18 00
160.. '' '' 1886 ..17	27 20
120.. '' '' 1887 ..17	20 40
240.. '' '' 1888 ..20	48 00
210..Representatives Cred's.. $\frac{3}{4}$	1 58
220..Alternates Credentials....$\frac{3}{4}$	1 65
170..Death reports.........o5	8 50
68..P. C. Tax Notices o1	68
84..Med. Exr. Credentials ..o3	2 52
130..Ass. Second Notices ,...o1	1 30
20..Ass. First Notices o1	20
95..Charter Lists ....$2\frac{1}{4}$	2 12
100..Deputy App. Notices....o1	1 00
90..Suspension Notices ......$\frac{3}{4}$	60

900..Ben. Cert. Blanks ......$1\frac{1}{2}$	13 50
182..Bonds o2	3 64
255..S A. Return Blanks o2	5 10
690..Disab. Benef.Ret.Blanks. $\frac{1}{2}$	3 45
190..Institution reports o2	3 80
50..Ode Cards o3	1 50
500..Constitutions o2	10 00
97..Disability proofs........o8	7 76
970..Beneficiary Ret. blanks.. $\frac{1}{2}$	4 85
6000..Warrant Blanks........66	3 96
6000..Rec. Treas Rect. blanks 66	3 96
6000..Treas. Rect. blanks 66	3 96
1172..Benf. Return '' 24-100	2 81
1 lot..Pamphlets	4 50
1..Supplies with DGC McWatt	8 75
1.. '' '' '' Stonehouse	8 .75
1.. '' '' '' Robson..	8 75
1.. '' '' '' Graham..	8 75
2..Rituals '' '' '' ..	2 00
3..S. A. Ret. Books........30	90
160..D.Gd.Cdrs Commissions o2	3 20
191..D.D.Gd Cdrs.Commissi's o2	3 82
1..Lot Roll book sheets	3 25
1..Ben. Register	5 00
22..Blankbooks 50	11 00

$8 372 47

REPORT OF THE FINANCE COMMITTEE.

To the Grand Commander, Officers and Comrades of the Grand Legion, of Ontario Select Knights of the A. O. U. W.

SIR AND COMRADES :—

Your Committee on Finance beg leave to submit the following report.

As the Grand Recorder's report contains detailed Statements of the Beneficiary and General Funds your Committee merely gives the total receipts and disbursements which are as follows :

Beneficiary Fund, including balance of 1888...$ 11307 00
Paid by Warrants 11307 00

Balance on hand April 1st, 1889...... Nil.

General Fund, including balance of $404.36
on hand May 1st 1888 ....$ 2962 88
Paid out by Warrants................................ 2555 54

Balance on hand April 1st, 1889 ...$ 407 34

The expenses of the year amounted to $2267.03. This includes the cost of the last annual session, which amounted to $535.27 and the sum of $150.00 for instituting new Legions.

It is satisfactory to note that all accounts against the Grand Legion have been paid to 1st inst. except two items of $12.50 each not due till June.

Your Committee have audited the books four times during the year as provided for by legislation of last session and have on every occasion found them correctly kept and with a minuteness of detail highly creditable to your Grand Recorder. To his untiring energy we attribute much of the success the Order has achieved and we hope that in the near future the onerous duties of Grand Recorder will be more adequately remunerated.

Your Committee would suggest that Grand Legion, when in session, inquire into the need existing in Grand Recorder's office of providing for the greater security of the rapidly accumulating documents, which, it is imperative, should be carefully preserved in a manner readily accessible for reference.

Your Committee would further suggest that the security bonds of the Grand Recorder and Grand Treasurer be for increased amounts.

Balance sheet, showing our financial standing on April 1st, 1889, is appended hereto.

All of which is fraternally submitted in E. I. & U.

JAMES WATT,
JOSEPH HARTON, ⎫ Finance Com.
GEO. WOLTZ,

TORONTO, April 15th, 1889.

Balance Sheet pro April 1st, 1889. .

DR.			CR.	
To Erin Legion No. 20 ....$	17	By Cash on hand.............$	407	34
" Victoria " " 27 ....'	1 73	" Office furniture	143	95
" Fergus " " 28	25	" Supplies in stock...........	372	47
" Royal " " 58	67	" Outstanding accounts	114	37
" Canadian Workman	12 50			
" " Overseer..........	12 50		$1038	13
Balance	1010 31			
	$1038 13	By Bal. in favor Grand Legion..$1010 31		

SIXTH ANNUAL REPORT

—OF THE—

Grand Medical Examiner,

SELECT KNIGHTS OF THE A. O. U. W.

TORONTO, 1ST APRIL, 1889.

*To the Grand Commander, Officers and Members of the Grand
Legion, Select Knights of the A. O. U. W. of Ontario.*

SIR AND COMRADES :—

I herewith submit my Sixth Annual Report.

The year is included from the 3rd day of May, 1888, to
the 31st day of March 1889, inclusive, in accordance with
legislation of last session. The report really only covers
eleven months.

The number of applications for the Ontario Beneficiary,
received and passed upon by me from the inception of the
scheme until the close of this report was 2002. The number
received and passed upon each year is herein recorded for
facility of reference, and comparison, as in previous reports;
and is as follows, viz :—

Number	1st	year	359
"	2nd	"	304
"	3rd	"	439
"	4th	"	320
"	5th	"	348
"	6th	"	232
		Total	2002

Of the 232 applications received the past year 205 were
approved on first examination, and 18 were rejected for various
causes. The remaining 9 were returned for correction, or additional information ; and of that number 8 were on second examination approved none rejected, but one has not been returned to my office.

(1)

APPLICATIONS REJECTED.

Following is the record of rejections the past year, together with the reasons therefor :

Case 1. Rejected on family history and personal condition, father died of lung disease—candidate's disparity in height and weight. Height 5ft. 8 in., and weight 116 lbs. Rejected by a sister society.

Case 2. Rejected on absence of family history; and personal condition. Local Examiner reports it a second class risk.

Case 3. Rejected on family history—candidate's mother and one brother died of Consumption.

Case 4. Rejected on family history. Mother died of Consumption. Local Examiner reports candidate a second class risk.

Case 5. Rejected on family history and local Examiner's report. Mother died of Cancer, one sister of Consumption, one of Typhoid Fever and one brother of the same disease.

Case 6. Rejected on personal history and condition of applicant. Applicant received a blow on the head in 1883, which caused him six months illness, confusion of mind, dimness of vision, unsteady gait, &c. Respiration 20 per minute and pulse 84. Nervous.

Case 7. Rejected on absence of family history—candidate had Congestion of Liver. Occupation stone cutter.

Case 8. Rejected on family history of Cancer and Heart Disease ; and disparity of height and weight of applicant. Height 5 ft. 10 in., weight 132 lbs.

Case 9. Rejected on account of being over age. The applicant was 50 years old on the 27th July, 1888, this application reached me on 31st August, 1888.

Case 10. Rejected on the grounds that applicant coul l not, or would not and did not give any information regarding either grand parents, parents, brothers or sisters.

Case 11. Rejected on personal history and condition : and local Examiner's report—disparity of height and weight. Height 6 ft. 1 in., weight 138 lbs. Rejected by a sister society.

Case 12. Rejected on personal history and condition. Chronic disease—unusually developed varicose veins of leg. Reported second class risk.

Case 13. Rejected on both family history and personal history and condition. Cause of father's death uncertain— personally abnormally contracted chest. Usual measurements not given. Not recommended by local Examiner.

Case 14. Rejected on family history and personal history and condition. One brother died of Consumption and another of contracted cold. Applicant suffers from Articular Rheumatism and nervous system lacks tone.

Case 15. Rejected on account of being over age. Applicant was 50 years old on 4th December '88, and application reached me on 17th December '88. The applicant was twice examined or certified, the last time on the 14th December '88, ten days after reaching 50 years of age.

Case 16. Rejected on family history and personal condition. Sister died of Consumption, the father died aged 42 years no cause assigned ; disparity between height and weight, height 5 ft. 8 in., weight 130.

Case 17. Rejected on family history, Father died of Bronchitis and Inflammatory Rheumatism at age of 40 years, mother at the same age of Inflammation of bowels ; one brother and one sister died of Consumption. Rejected by a sister society.

Case 18. Rejected on family history. Of the brothers and sisters two died of Consumption and one of inflammation of the lungs.

The number of rejections the past year was in excess of the preceding year, though the number of applications was less. There cannot of course be any ratio calculated between the two. This fact however must be borne in mind that the Select Knights membership is largely made up of members of advanced age, and that sooner or later the death rate must increase. I claim therefore that I have but jealously guarded the Beneficiary Department against the admission of any but first-class risks, so far as I have been able, with the evidence before me, to judge. At the same time I have not knowingly done any applicant any injustice. In all cases where there was any doubt I have given the order the benefit of the doubt.

SOURCE OF APPLICATIONS.

The applications received from the various Legions were as follows, viz.:—

No.	Name of Legion.	No. of Applic'ns.	No.	Name of Legion.	No. of Applic'ns.
1	Lincoln	1	42	Collingwood	None.
2	Niagara Falls	1	43	Durham	3
3	Wentworth	3	44	Empress	None.
4	Union	None.	45	Waterloo	None.
5	Star	1	46	Mystic	1
6	Toronto	2	47	Lyn	4
7	Cooksville	None.	48	Rideau	None.
8	Seguin	None.	49	Ontario	None.
9	Bradford	None.	50	Jamieson	None.
10	Kingston	5	51	Simcoe	None.
11	Lynden	None.	52	Queen City	6
12	Iroquois	None.	53	Crystal	6
13	Jarvis	None.	54	Tottenham	2
14	Picton	None.	55	Tamworth	None.
15	Caledonia	1	56	Centreville	None.
15	Kempenfeldt	4	57	Queensville	4
17	Frontier	None.	58	Royal	None.
18	Wellington	4	59	Norfolk	3
19	Tilsonburg	None.	60	Morpeth	1
20	Erin	None.	61	Howard	None.
21	Excelsior	1	62	Banner	2
22	Phœnix	1	63	Elmvale	1
23	York	4	64	Belleville	3
24	Lennox	1	65	Lake	5
25	Equity	None.	66	Dunn	5
26	Leopold	2	67	Dundas	3
27	Victoria	None.	68	Hickcox	1
28	Fergus	None.	69	Niagara	None.
29	Fenton	1	70	Brampton	None.
30	Shelburne	2	71	Fidelity	1
31	Morrisburg	1	72	Hillsburg	None.
32	Island	1	73	Lorne	1
33	Capital	10	74	Marine	3
34	Orillia	None.	75	*Lisgar	17
35	Eglinton	None.	76	*Caledon	12
36	Whitby	1	77	*Schomberg	15
37	Stanhoff	None.	78	*Kingsville	28
38	Dufferin	7	79	*Grenville	12
39	Kemptville	None.	80	*Stanley	3
40	Gordon	None.	1	Pioneer, Q	12
41	Muskoka	1	2	Stadacona, Q	22

NOTE.—Those indicated with an asterisk are the Legions which were organized since last Report, as far as they have forwarded applications to me. J. S. K.

Of the 76 Legions on my list at the beginning of the year, no less than 34 or nearly one half sent in no applications for the Beneficiary. From the remaining 42 Legions there were received 146 or an average of less than 3½ from each Legion a decrease as compared with the previous year.

The six new Legions aggregated 86 applications, an average of about 14⅓ to each new Legion. Here again we have a decrease in the number of the new Legions, number of applications and in the average to each Legion.

Only one conclusion can be drawn from the consideration of these facts—the area of supply must be extended. The Order of Select Knights should no longer occupy the position of the child dependent on the parent; but develop its manhood and independence. It will then be no longer handicapped in the race among beneficiary societies. It will gain youth and vigor instead of drafting alone from those at or near the meridian of life and who have already in many cases all the insurance they require or all they can afford, and bring down the rate of mortality to a point as low as can be reasonably expected by human anticipation of life's probabilities.

THE QUESTION OF AGE.

It will be interesting and at the same time instructive to note in this connection, as in former years the ages of applicants. As heretofore I have grouped the ages in series of five years each.

From 21 to 25 years of age inclusive .... 8 applicants.
" 26 to 30 " " " ....17 "
" 31 " 35 " " " ....31 "
" 36 " 40 " " " ....40 "
" 41 " 45 " " " ....60 "
" 46 " 50 " " " ....75 "

Total........................ 232

The average age of the 232 was 40. 78 years, the average last year being 40. 53 years—a slight increase over last year.

Over one-half applied after the age of ....42 years.
About one third " " " ....45 "
Nearly one-fourth " " " ....47 "
One in each 4⅓ " at or over the age of ....48 "
One eighth applied at or over the age of ....49 "

To secure a low death rate, we must attain a lower average age of admission. The average between 21 and 50 years is 35. 50, while the average shown as our admissions is 40. 78. Now we cannot reasonably hope to reach a lower average than 35. 50, though it is not impossible provided the source of supply will enable us to reach the minimum admission at 21 years and secure material not already loaded up with insurance.

OCCUPATION OF APPLICANTS.

Farmers were the most numerous there being... 55 applic'ts
Merchants and Manufacturers, follow next with... 53 "
Of Tradesmen and Laboring men there were...... 34 "
Contractors, Speculators, Agents, & Managers. .... 24 "
Accountants, Bookkeepers, Sec'ys, Clerks, Salesmen 21 "
Professional Men and Journalists .... 17 "
Engaged in manufacture or sale of Liquors ...... 6 "
Retired or without occupation .... 4 "
Miscellaneous occupations .... 18 "

232

HEIGHT AND WEIGHT.

With reference of height—all applicants except 35 stood within the 6 inches range of 5 feet 6 inches to within 6 feet. Of the 35, no less that 20 were under 5 feet 6 inches, the shortest being 5 feet 4 inches. Of the tall men 15 stood 6 feet or over. The tallest applicant being 6 feet 4 inches.

In the matter of weights there was considerable diversity. The heaviest weighed 256 lbs., the lightest 110 lbs. Of the remainder

3 applicants weighed from...............111 to 120 pounds.
11 " " " ....121 to 130 "
46 " " " ....131 to 140 "
34 " " " ....141 to 150 "
44 " " " ....151 to 160 "
28 " " " ....161 to 170 "
29 " " " ....171 to 180 "
19 " " " ....181 to 190 "
8 " " " ....191 to 200 "
8 " " " ....over 200.

LIQUOR AND TOBACCO USERS.

Of the 232 applicants
     67 used neither liquor nor tobacco.
     78 " both liquor and tobacco.
     25 " liquor only.
     62 " tobacco only.

Total using liquor was 103.

Total using tobacco was 140.

This is a record now made for the third time ; and which I hope to see continued for a series of years and which may in time prove valuable in determining the influence of liquor and tobacco on health, or longevity.

DEATH REGISTER YEAR ENDING 31st MARCH, 1889.

No. of Death.	Names and Occupations.	Age on Admission	Legion and No.	Reg. No.	Date Application approved.	Date of Death.	Duration of Membership.	Cause of Death.	REMARKS.
20	J. E. Browse.... (Physician)	44	Island No. 32 ..	555	Feb. 7th 1885.	April 18th 1888.	3 y. 2 m. 11 d.	Congestion of the Brain.	Confined to bed 2¼ weeks.
21	John G. Strachan (P. O. Clerk)	51	Kingston No, 10..	81	Sept. 20th 1883	May 8th 1888.	4 y. 7 m. 18 d.	Catarrhal Pneumonia.	Ill 6 days.
22	John McDonald... (Foreman)	49	Wentworth No. 3	942	Feb. 18th 1886	May 8th 1888.	2 y. 2 m. 20 d.	Pneumonia.	Ill 4 weeks.
23	Alex. A Reid . (Book Keeper)	50	Wentworth No. 3	141	Oct. 27th 1883.	July 1st 1888.	4 y. 8 m. 4 d.	Congestion of the Brain.	Ill one month.
24	Thos. Holder .... (Gardiner.)	34	Banner No. 62 ..	1265	Sept. 25th 1886	July 12th 1888.	1 y. 9 m. 19 d.	Tumor in Brain.	Ill six months.
25	C, G, Barnes.... (Salesman)	48	York No. 23	903	June 25th 1885.	Dec. 15th 1888.	3 y. 5 m. 20 d.	Meningitis.	Ill 2 weeks.

Referring to the foregoing table, it would appear that the average length of membership of those who died during the past year was about 3 years and 4 months. The record of six deaths during the year or 25 deaths in six years is one on which Grand Legion may be congratulated.

A DISABILITY CLAIM.

I have received the past year one claim under the Disability clause of the constitution. The papers reached me on the 6th March, 1889. The claimant received his degree in the Legion on the 30 March, 1887, and was reported to me at the time as a first class risk with no heart trouble or other ailment. The claim was supported by the officers of his Legion and by three doctors. One doctor reported that the claimant had valvular disease of the heart, tumor of the left testicle, and a malignant growth or tumor in the abdomen, as causing the total disability. A second doctor gave a report similar to the foregoing; while a third by Dr. West the Legion Doctor in addition reported as follows, viz :—

"He has been under my care for almost a year now. "His present disability in my opinion may be put down as "being traceable to injuries sustained by slipping while lifting "a rail in an awkward position. Since that time a tumor "(abdominal) has made its appearance, also a tumefied condi- "tion of one of the testicles. His peculiar cachetic appearance "and other correlative symptoms lead me to believe that to be "cancerous tumors. He had albuminuria when last I examin- "ed the urine and also valvular trouble in the heart. Hence "I recommend him as a totally disabled, aye, a doomed man."

My decision was given in the following words, viz :—

"This case is one induced by disease rather than accident. "By constitution Art. XI, Sec's 1 and 5, no distinction is made "as to cause ; and I am left no option, so long as total disa- "bility is proven, which is proven in this case. I therefore ap- "prove the validity of the claim."

I have to point out the desirability if not the necessity of some action on the part of the Grand Legion to settle the question of what is to be considered total disability ; and whether such shall be made dependent upon disease, as well as accident. If so whenever a disease such as consumption or in fact any other which is likely to end in death, seizes a member, such member may claim under the law as it now stands inasmuch as he cannot work.

CONCLUSION.

In concluding this report I have to thank not only the various local Examiners for their usually painstaking examinations and judicious recommendations, but both medical Examiners and Legion Recorders for supplying me with additional information when appealed to.

Congratulating the membership on their immunity from payment of assessments; and trusting that my efforts to maintain a high standard of health for admission to the Beneficiary Department will meet your approval, I remain,

Yours fraternally,

JOHN S. KING, M. D.,

Grand Medical Examiner S. K.

APPENDIX.

Report of the D. G. C. for the Province of Quebec.

W. J. PORTE, Grand Commander, S. K. of the A. O. U. W.

Dear Sir and Comrade :—In submitting this my first annual report as D. G. C. for the Province of Quebec. I have deemed it wise not to endeavor to institute new Legions but to encourage a more healthy and stronger growth of those already in existence, and I have labored towards that end, for I found on broaching the advisability of an additional Legion here was met with sentiments of the strongest disapproval.

The attendance and interest manifested in the meetings of both Pioneer and Stadacona Legions has been most encouraging until their membership having increased sufficiently. There is now every prospect of two strong and prosperous Legions being instituted shortly as a Charter List has been started with twelve good names attached, also, one in St. Johns with eighteen names which if allowed to be instituted will without doubt become some of the best Legions in the Province, as they will be composed of some of the most energetic and live members of the A. O. U. W. Trusting the present session of this Grand Legion will prove the most enjoyable of any yet held.

I submit this in E. I. & U.,

J. J. ULLEY, D. G. C. for Province of Quebec.

Montreal, Que., April 19th, 1889.

Report of the D. G. C. for South Simcoe.

W. J. PORTE, ESQ., Grand Commander.

Dear Sir and Comrade:—In making this my third annual report as Deputy Grand Commander I am unable to report any increase of new Legions in my District. In fact there is no room for any as I have put a Legions in all the A. O. U. W. Lodges in my District that could sustain them. This year my business confined me to such an extent that I was unable to visit the adjoining counties, where some Legions might perhaps be opened if exertions were made. I have visited several of the Legions in my district and installed their officers. Would have visited more of them, only the roads being so bad last Fall and Winter. While the Legions in my district are not rapidly increasing in membership, still they are not decreasing. I feel sorry that our brethren of the A. O. U. W. are not giving us the helping hand they should and in a large number of instances join other societies. I hope that at the approaching session of Grand Legion steps will be taken whereby a more rapid growth of our membership is secured.

Thanking you for the honor you have conferred upon me by appointing me as your Deputy, I desire in conclusion to express my sincere thanks to the Comrades in my district for the kindness they have extended to me when visiting their Legions.

Fraternally in E. I. & U.,

W. R. FENTON, D. G. C. for South Simcoe.

Report of the D. D. G. C. for Grenville County.

W. J PORTE, Grand Commander, S. K. of the A. O. U. W.

Dear Sir and Brother:—In making this my first annual report as your D. D. G. C., I am pleased to inform you that the Legions in this County are in a very prosperous condition, adding to their number slowly and surely.

I have not been called upon to perform any official duty other than installing officers in my own Legion.

Thanking you for the honor you have conferred upon me to act as D.D.G.C. for this County.

I remain,   Yours fraternally in E. I. & U.,

W. G. ROBINSON, D. D. G. C. for County Grenville.

Prescott, April 20th, 1889.

Report of the D. D. G. C. for Addington County.

W. J. PORTE, ESQ., Grand Commander, S. K. of the A. O. U. W.

Dear Sir and Comrade :—Tamworth Legion No. 55, like Tamworth Lodge A. O. U. W., has during the past year remained *in statu quo.*

There is a very general feeling of confidence in the Order—much more so than a year ago—and the prospect seems brighter for increase in membership, there being just now a revival in the A. O. U. W. Lodge from which we hope for good things for the S. K's.

I have but this one Legion under my jurisdiction. The membership is 20, all holding Grand Legion Beneficiary Certificates.

Fraternally yours,

JAS. AYLSWORTH, D. D. G. C. for Addington.

Tamworth, April 12th, 1889.

Report of the D. D. Gd. Cdr. for the City of Montreal.

W. J. PORTE, ESQ., Grand Commander, S. K. of the A. O. U. W.

Dear Sir and Comrade :—With my respects of to-day I have the honor of reporting to you that since my assuming the office of D. D. G. C. in June last. succeeding Comrade W. D. McLaren, Jr., whom you were pleased to appoint to the office of Grand Marshall, I have made three official visits to each, "Pioneer" and "Stadacona" Legions. The increase in membership during the year just closing is very marked; the "Pioneers" having ad led 15 members, with one application on hand, while the "Stadaconas" took into their ranks 34 members and have 9 applications to report upon at the May meeting. This result is the more gratifying when true regard is had to the facts that both Legions were instituted by Comrade B. J. Leubsdorf, D. G. C. at the end of March, 1888, and are consequently, but thirteen months old. The circumstances as well as obstacles surrounding the order of the S. K's in this Province necessitate the exercise of patience and foresight in building up this branch of the A. O. U. W., but within a very short time this district will have another Legion, as Stanley Lodge, which has already a splendid record, is indefatigable in forming a Legion, and the number of charter members exceeds already the required quota.

My financial report I have made to our Comrade the Grand Recorder, at intervals.

In accordance with the duties devolving upon me I installed the officers of Stadacona Legion on January 3rd, those of Pioneer Legion on January 10th, 1889, and it affords me pleasure to state that much interest is taken in the work.

During my term of office I have had but one important question to deal with, and my opinion on which you heartily concurred in.

In conclusion I beg leave to thank you for courtesies extended to me, and I ask you to accept the assurance of my sincere salutation with which I remain.

Yours fraternally in E. I. & U.,

E. W. BEUTHNER, D. D. G. C.

Montreal, April 20th, 1889.

[XI]

Report of the D. D. G. C. for Dundas County.

W. J. PORTE ESQ. Grand Commander, S. K. of A. O. U. W.

Dear Sir and Comrade :—In obedience to the constitution I have the honor of submitting my annual report of the work done during my term of office. I have instituted three Legions they are all in good working order and are increasing in membership, although not as rapidly as I would wish to see. I have been in constant correspondence with a number of Lodges in this vicinity as to the formation of Legions, I think there can be a few more good Legions instituted during the coming year.

Thanking you Grand Commander for my appointment, also the kindness, courtesy and promptness of the Grand Recorder on all occasions.

I am, Yours fraternally in E. I. & U.

C. ROBSON, D. D. G C., for Dundas County.

Iroquois, April 18th, 1889.

Report of the D. D. G. C. for Norfolk County.

W. J. PORTE, Grand Commander, S. K. of the A. O. U. W.

Dear Sir and Comrade :—In accordance with the Constitution, I beg leave to submit my report for the limit to which I was appointed D. D. Gd. Commander, viz : the County of Norfolk.

As yet there is only the one Legion instituted in the County that of Norfolk Legion No. 59. located at Simcoe. There has been a small increase added to the membership this term, but not to that extent which we may have desired.

It seems a difficult matter to make much progress, and I trust an extra effort may be made by the Grand Legion at its coming session to bring the order more prominently before the brethren in the A. O. U. W.

It is very gratifying to see that the Order has been so highly favored regarding its death rate, thus showing that a strict medical examination is our only safe guard. If such is continued and more life can be put into the Order I see no reason why the membership should not be considerably increased.

Yours in E. I. & U.,

J. THOS. MURPHY, D. D. G. C.

Simcoe, April 20th, 1889.

Report of the D. D. G. C. for North Simcoe.

W. J. PORTE, Grand Commander, S. K. of the A. O. U. W.

Comrades :—In presenting this my annual report I have much pleasure in stating that the Order is making steady progress in this District.

In February last I visited Elmvale Legion No. 63 and installed the officers, I found the Legion in a prosperous condition and the officers well skilled in their drill and work.

Collingwood Legion is also progressing very well, they have regular meetings both for drill and work. the former is taught by a professional instructor and they are now discussing the propriety of purchasing uniforms.

I have not been called on to hear or settle any disputes in the District during my term of office.

All of which is fraternally submitted,

JOHN NETTLETON, D. D. G. C. for North Simcoe.

Collingwood, April 18th, 1889,

Report of the D. D. G. C. for Carleton County.

W. J. PORTE, Grand Commander, S. K. of the A. O. U. W.

Dear Sir and Comrade :—I beg leave to report that the prospects of the Order in this District is now very good ; there is yet but one Legion in this District, but am confident that we will soon have another at Carleton place.

Capital Legion No. 33 has done good work this last year and has every prospect of still doing better, every member now joining gets his Beneficiary in our Department and all are extra well pleased both with the work and cost·

This Legion has visited the three city Lodges in uniform, by appointment, when the aim and object of the Order was given several propositions were received.

Thanking you for the honor conferred upon me as D. D. G. C.

I remain yours in E. I. & U.,

JAS. J. HAMILTON, D. D. G. C. for Carleton.

Ottawa, April 22nd, 1889.

Report of D. D G. C. for South Simcoe.

J. PORTE, Grand Commander, S. K. of the A. O. U. W.

Dear Sir and Comrade :—I am not able to make a report as I should as I did not attend any meetings of the Legion in my District last year. I had no way to go and I found the Legions were working well under our D. G. Comrade Fenton and it was not much use in my visiting them. I would suggest a few changes to or ought to be made at next Grand Legion meeting, 1st that all Legion of Select Knights have power to give the 2 degrees on one, and the same evening, 2nd that the Select Knights be separated from the A. O. U. W. it would give the Select Knights more strength and would work a great deal better and produce a large improvement in membership I think.

I am yours fraternally in E. I. & U.,

ROBERT HENDERSON, D. D. G. C. for South Simcoe.

Alliston, April 22nd, 1889.

Report of the D. D. G. C. for York County.

W. J. PORTE, Grand Commander. S. K. of the A. O. U. W.

Dear Sir and Comrade :—In submitting this my report as D. D. G. C. of York. Allow me on the outset to thank you for the appointment which I never sought for, and I regret that Comrade Wyndow was unable to attend to same owing to business matters. I may say that I have visited all the City Legions on more than one occasion ; also that I have installed the officers of the different Legions and have had the hearty support of Comrades from different Legions in furnishing me with guard of honor for which I return my sincere thanks, I may say that the best of good feelings exists with all the Legions. I regret that the different Legions have not been taking in so much material as I would have liked, but things are changing and material is coming in fairly well, in all the Legions in the city, particularly in Crystal, where I purpose making my last official visit on 23rd inst, when we are to have 10 or 12 candidates for that evening.

I have granted two dispensations for conferring both degrees the same evening, and forwarded the same to B. J. Leubsdorf, G. R., amounting to $1.00. I have to return my sincere thanks to you and also to other Grand Legion Officers for their attendance at A. O. U. W. concert held in Toronto February last.

Queen City Legion desired me to hold an open installation I granted request, and think it would be wise for other Legions to copy their example. In conclusion I would thank all the Comrades in the city of Toronto for their kind services and good wishes, and if I have been instrumental in doing any good for our Order, the fact of knowing it will amply repay me for same.

I am, fraternally yours in E. I. &. U.,

WM. J. GRAHAM, D. D. G. C., for York.

Toronto, April 15th, 1889.

[XIII]

Report of the D. D. G. C. for Wentworth County.

Wm. J. PORTE, Grand Commander, S. K. of the A. O. U. W.

I have the honor to report that I as D. D. G. C. for the County of Wentworth installed the officers of Mystic Legion No. 46, on January 8th, 1889, and of Wentworth Legion 3, on January 22nd, 1889, after which on each occasion I addressed them in the interest of the Order; setting forth the very cheap insurance aud all the other advantages of the S. K.. I have not absented myself from a meeting only about twice since I was a member of the Order, that is four years ago, of either my own Legion or Wentworth Legion not only as a member but as an officer for I have been in harness from the inception and never lost an opportunity to advance the interest and welfare of the Order, but I must admit that we have not met with the success that I so much *desire* yet I am pleased to report that as you are aware there has not been a death among our members the past year and also that Mystic Legion has one new member and Wentworth has two applications.

I must give you my opinion that the future success of our Order not only largely depends upon but that it is absolutely necessary for our very existence as every person that knows anything about insurance and what is necessary to keep life in any society is the constantly adding to their membership and as we can only get our membership from the A. O. U. W. and taking into consideration the very small per centage of their members that belong to the S. K. I have come to the conclusion that separation is the only thing that will save us. Why should we stand by and let new societies spring up in our midst and yet, as they do,, more of the A. O. U. W. members to join them than are members of the S. K.

I have the honor to be yours in E. I. &. U.,

JAS. H. SHOULDICE, D. D. G. C. County of Wentworth.

Hamilton, April 18th, 1889.

Report of the D. D. G. C. for Ontario County.

W. J. PORTE, Grand Commander, S. K. of the A. O. U. W.

Dear Sir and Comrade :—As D. D. for Ontario County, I beg leave to submit the following Report, and regret being unable to present a more favorable one. There are only two Legions in this district Equity, No. 25, (Oshawa) and Whitby No. 36, through unavoidable causes I have not been able to visit the former as often as I wished, and on my official visit in February last, I found the Legion in a very unhealthy condition, as they frequently cannot get a quorum owing to a number of the Comrades having left the town, consequently their business has to be done in a very informal manner.

I suggested the propriety of either giving up their Charter and offiliating with Durham or Whitby, or stirring up the brethren there to join the S. K. they pledged themselves to the latter, but as yet I have not heard of any new applications.

My own Legion is not I regret to say prospering as much as I would desire, we have only added one new member during the past year, for which I granted a dispensation to confer the two degrees the same evening, the fee for which was forwarded to the G. R. at the time. (January)

I attribute the want of prosperity in this district, first to the too numerous societies of a similiar beneficiary nature, and secondly to that "bugbear" uniform.

I feel that I have somewhat failed in my duty to the Order, but I can assure you it was not for want of a little "enthuse" and I trust my successor will find this District much more prosperous in another year.

Thanking you sir for the honor conferred upon me, and with all good wishes and faith in our Order, I remain,

Yours fraternally, in E. I, & U..

R. S. CORMACK, D. D. G. C., Ontario County.

Whitby, April 17th, 1889.

Report of the D. D. G. C. for Frontenac County.

W. J. PORTE, ESQ., Grand Commander.

Dear Sir and Comrade :—I beg to report on the progress of our Legion No. 10, Kingston. That during the year we have lost one of our best members Comrade J. G. Strachan, who died on the 8th day of May 1888, which was a great loss to our Legion ; as he was always ready to help the Legion.

During the year of 1888 and 1889 we had the pleasure to initiate six good men into our Legion of S. K. all of which took Beneficiary Certificates. Also I have granted five dispensations for five of the Comrades J. A. Dermet, S. J. Kirpatrick, T. J. Hempton, Wm. Drennan. A. V. Lykes, all of which are good men. We have six applications in now, all of which have passed our Medical Examiner and will be forwarded to the Grand Medical Examiner for his approval, I hope this year will be a year of prosperity and that by the end of 1889 the Select Knights of the A. O. U. W. will be able to pay Two Thousand Dollars.

I beg to remain yours fraternally in E. I. &. U.,

W. K. ROUTLEY, D. D. G. C. for Frontenac County.

Kingston May 4th, 1889.